The Crowning Day

LIST OF ORGANISATIONS WITH WHICH
HARRY IRONSIDE WAS ASSOCIATED

Africa Inland Mission - President
American Association for Jewish Evangelism
    Chairman, Advisory Board
American Scripture Gift Mission
    Member, Board of Reference
William Jennings Bryan College
    Member, Board of Directors
Central American Mission
    Member, Board of Directors
Christ for America
    Member, Board of Reference
Dallas Theological Seminary
    Member, Board of Regents
Bob Jones University
    Member, Board of Directors
Montrose Bible Conference Association
    Director and Member, Board of Directors
Moody Bible Institute - Member, Board of Directors
Overseas Missionary Fellowship (formerly China
    Inland Mission) - Member; North American
    Council
Southern Bible Training School
    Chairman, Board of Directors
Western Book and Tract Company - President
Wheaton College (Illinois)
    Member, Board of Directors
Winona Lake Bible Conference
    Member, Board of Directors

Dr. Harry Ironside

That day lies hid
that every day we be on
the watch

- Augustine

The Crowning Day

FOUR GOLDEN HOURS
At Kingsway Hall, London

with

DR. HARRY IRONSIDE
Pastor, Moody Memorial Church, Chicago

AMBASSADOR

The Crowning Day

ISBN 0 907927 89 0

First Ambassador Edition 1993

AMBASSADOR PRODUCTIONS LTD.
Providence House
16 Hillview Avenue,
Belfast, BT5 6JR
Northern Ireland

To
The Memory Of
Joe Donnelly
This Book Is Affectionately Dedicated

I never begin my work in the morning without thinking that perhaps He may interrupt my work and begin His own. I am not looking for death, I am looking for Him.

- G. Campbell Morgan

Our Lord is now rejected
And by the world disowned:
By the many still neglected,
And by the few enthroned;
But soon He'll come in glory!
The hour is drawing nigh,
For the crowning day is coming
By and by.

O the crowning day is coming,
Is coming by and by,
When our Lord shall come in 'power'
And 'glory' from on high!
O the glorious sight will gladden
Each waiting, watchful eye,
In the crowning day that's coming
By and by.

The heavens shall glow with splendour;
But brighter far than they,
The saints shall shine in glory,
As Christ shall them array:
The beauty of the Saviour
Shall dazzle every eye
In the crowning day that's coming
By and by.

Our pain shall then be over;
We'll sin and sigh no more;
Behind us all of sorrow,
And naught but joy before-
A joy in our Redeemer,
As we to Him are nigh
In the crowning day that's coming
By and by.

Let all that look for hasten
The joyful coming day
By earnest consecration,
To walk the narrow way;
By gathering in the lost ones
For whom our Lord did die,
For the crowning day that's coming
By and by.

Daniel Webster Whittle

I am daily wating for the coming of the Son of God

George Whitefield

INTRODUCTION

Dr. Ironside's addresses at Kingsway as published in this volume expounded the Scriptures which tell how the Second Coming of Christ will affect the Jews, the Gentiles, and the Church of God.

With unqualified agreement with the views expressed, we heartily commend them to all who desire to know how God will fulfil His purpose of redeeming love and glorify and vindicate His beloved Son "Whom He hath appointed heir of all things, by whom also He made the worlds. Who being the brightness of His glory and the express image of His person when He had by Himself purged our sins sat down at the right hand of the majesty on high."

It says much for the great interest in the truth of the Second Advent and of the renown of Dr. Ironside as well as not a little for the earnestness of whose who organised the meetings at Kingsway Hall, that it was only about a fortnight before the Doctor was returning home to America that it became known that he had a few days in which he could speak in London if arrangements were possible at such short notice.

It was felt that we should be the losers if we did not benefit by the Doctor's great experience and knowledge of "things to come". It seemed also that so distinguished a teacher ought not to leave England without a word of welcome and Godspeed from us.

Knowing how difficult it is to organise meetings in this great city at short notice, we were cast upon God, and after much prayer the great Kingsway Hall was taken in faith and a few of the Lord's devoted servants met to determine how best to reach the thousands of people necessary to fill the hall. Willing help was offered and for two weeks the results of our efforts were in the balance. But we need have had, and indeed we had not, any fear. For God rewarded our faith by filling the Hall every night and a wonderful time of joy and thanksgiving was spent and the Lord was glorified.

Now this verbatim report of the addresses is sent out in the hope that the words of the truth of the Gospel, already heard by the thousands who were present at the meetings, will bring enlightenment and hope to very many more.

F.W.Pitt

CONTENTS

FOUR GOLDEN HOURS

I

THE COMING OF OUR LORD JESUS CHRIST

I CAN hardly say how much I appreciate the very undeserved privilege of standing here to-night to present to you something concerning the Coming Again of our Lord Jesus Christ in this place where so many mighty men of God have borne testimony throughout the years. I am quite sure of this, that I cannot really add anything to what they have already proclaimed. I have not anything new to bring to you ; if I had, it would not be true. For, you know, in regard to God's truth whatever is true is not new, and whatever is new is not true. Ours is " the faith once for all delivered to the saints." The most I can hope to do is to " stir up your pure minds by way of remembrance," that is, those of you who are already looking for the Coming of our Lord Jesus Christ, and " our gathering together unto Him," and who are looking for His Return to the earth as the one means of solving all earth's problems.

I have no doubt that the great majority of this splendid audience to-night is made up of real Convention people. At least I take it that you over here are very much like us in America. You know, if we have a Convention of any kind in the Moody Church we can always depend on about 3,000 regular meeting folk; they always come; they are always interested; they are always there to stand by anything that they believe to be of God. Then if we can get in a sprinkling of the less-interested people, we are very thankful. To-night I want to address myself not to the regular folk, to you who are prophetic adepts—I am going to talk to you—but I shall be thinking more particularly of any friends who have come in here to-night who have never yet given very much attention to the doctrine of the Second Advent of our Lord Jesus Christ. There are, in fact, a great many professed Christians who have not given much attention to it. In a general way they believe in it, but just what is involved in the doctrine of the Second Advent they do no know.

I remember on one occasion I was asked to give an address at a ministers' meeting in a Canadian city; I do not want to particularize too carefully. After I had finished my address the meeting was thrown open for discussion, and I soon found that those who looked at things as I did were very much in the minority. One splendid man was asked to speak on the subject; he was a man widely known; he had written a great many books, and I had read every one of them, and I was exceedingly glad to meet him. He was asked if he would not say something as to what he thought of the doctrine of the Second Coming. He was very courteous. He said, " I am really sorry you have asked me to say anything, because the fact of the matter is, I never like disagreeing with a guest speaker; but since you have put me on the spot, I simply have to say that, while I appreciate the spirit of our friend (that was very kind of him), I do not believe a word he says. I cannot accept his view. Now do not misunderstand me. I do not believe in the Second Advent of our Lord Jesus Christ. There must be something about it in the Bible, or we would not have the Advent Lessons in the Prayer Book. But just what is meant by it I do not know, and I have never met anyone else that did; and I am certain our visitor does not know either, though he believes he does. I give him credit for being thoroughly honest. There is something terrific about this idea of the Second

Advent of Christ to me, and I cannot understand people who talk about it in such a free and easy way, and who seem so eager to see it take place. If I believed that the Saviour might return to-morrow, I should not be able to sleep to-night for anxiety. And just imagine a clergyman starting out to visit his parishioners on a given day, and the awful thought coming to him, ' The Lord may be here to-day ! ' Why, it would just paralyse Christian effort. I know, speaking for myself, I would want to get back to my study, and get down on my knees, and cry to God to make me fit for that great event. The way our friend has spoken about it to me is perfectly appalling. Why, he has intimated to us that if the Lord should come even to-day, all the saints would be caught up to meet Him ; and whatever would become of the rest of us poor fellows ? It is perfectly appalling."

This, of course, put me in rather a difficult position, for I was a much younger man than he was ; yet I felt I had to be faithful, and I said, "I do hope you do not mean that a man could have been a clergyman for, say, fifty years in the great historical Church of which you are a member, and have taken all the various ecclesiastical and academical degrees, and received ecclesiastical recognition in so many different ways, and yet had never been washed from his sins in the precious blood of Christ ? Surely you do not mean that. You know, doctor, if you have, as I hope you have, and as I trust you have, been washed in the blood of Jesus, well, when the saints are caught up, you will be caught up as well ; and you will get great light in prophetic truth all in a moment."

There are lots of people like that man ; and I am thinking of those who love the Lord, but who, somehow or another, have never looked into this subject ; and I am not surprised. Some of them think that it is largely either a kind of fanaticism on the one hand, or else just a wild emotionalism on the other. Yet what doctrine is there that has the place in the Word of God that this doctrine has, or what doctrine has a greater place in the Word ? Some years ago Dr. A. J. Gordon collated the texts in the New Testament on this subject, and he found that one verse in every twenty-five has to do with the Second Coming of Christ. When I read that— and it was about forty years ago—I said, well, if that is true, from now on I must preach at least one sermon in twenty-five on this subject ; that is the least I can do. I started to try to do that, and I soon found that there were so many hungry folk who wanted to know more about it that I

found myself pressed to preach on it a great many
more times, and some people began to think that
I was a kind of crank on the Second Coming.
But I am not ; I am perfectly sober ; I am not a
fanatic, but some folks thought I was because I
preached on the subject in about one sermon out
of five ; and I have never felt like apologizing,
because I am trying to make up for so many of
my brethren who never preach on it at all ; so
you cannot be surprised if I say more about it
than I would do ordinarily.   To me it is not just
a doctrine. The reason I love to speak of it is
this. My friend of Calvary is coming back again,
the One who loved me even unto death, the One
who sticketh closer than a brother, who went to
the Cross and died that He might put away my
sin, and who said before He went away, " I go
to prepare a place for you, and if I go and prepare a place for you I will come again, and receive
you unto Myself, that where I am, there ye may
be also." He won my heart forty-seven years
ago ; He saved my soul, and I will never be fully
satisfied till I see Him as He is.   And I am waiting
for that day when " the heavens shall glow with
splendour " and the Blessed Lord " will descend
from Heaven with a shout, with the voice of the
archangel, and with the trump of God, and the
dead in Christ shall rise first, and we which are

alive and remain shall be caught up together to meet the Lord in the air."

I want to speak to you on three verses in Matthew xxi, verses 42 to 44. Our Lord Jesus Christ was already within the shadow of the Cross. In a few more days He was to be rejected and crucified ; He was to die for our sins. And, of course, He came into the world for that very purpose. He said, " The Son of Man came not to be ministered unto, but to minister, and to give His life a ransom for many." Nevertheless, man is guilty before God for His rejection. The apostle Peter, you remember, said afterwards : " Him, being delivered by the determinate counsel and foreknowledge of God, ye have taken, and by wicked hands have crucified and slain." The Lord Jesus knew exactly what was to take place ; nothing ever took Him by surprise. I went into a book-store in Philadelphia one day, it was a Christian book-store, and I picked up a book that shocked me. I turned over a few pages, and I came across a sermon on " The Rashness of Jesus." The preacher pointed out that young men are very much inclined to be rash, and unduly to put themselves into places of danger. He was preaching on Jesus setting His face steadfastly to go to Jerusalem. It seemed such a pity, according to this preacher, that the Lord should have done that. He had a group of friends about Him in Galilee, and the people were becoming more and more acquainted with Him, and learning to love Him. And if only He had been content to stay there in Capernaum, why He might have founded a college there, and He might have had students come, not only from all over Palestine, but eventually from all over the world ; they would have thronged there. They came to sit at the feet of the various philosophers, and they might have come and sat at His feet. And suppose He had lived to be sixty, seventy, or eighty years of age, and had become a venerable and respected Teacher, and had instructed thousands of people, why the history of the world would have been changed ! These students of His could have gone out to carry His message of goodwill to men all over the globe. And then, too, if He had only settled down, as He grew older and became more mature, He could have put His thoughts into writing, and He might have produced a wonderful literature, and all the libraries of the earth would have been enriched by books which Jesus had written, for He could have written such wonderful things. But no, He could not be content ; He was so rash. The very fact that He knew they wanted to kill Him down in Jerusalem was a challenge to

Him, and He felt He must go and face it out, and, perhaps, make them come to His way of thinking.

I thought of the blasphemy, and the wretched delusion of it. Why, He knew all things. He came all the way from the glory to the manger at Bethlehem for the express purpose of " giving His life a ransom " for our sins ; and He said, " No man taketh My life from Me. I have power to lay it down, and I have power to take it again." And until His hour had come no weapon formed against Him could possibly have prospered. Yet, you know, although that is true, it does not do away with the sin of those who rejected and spurned Him, and hurried Him to the Cross, even though He went voluntarily there to die on our behalf.

So, foreseeing all that, He related this parable, and He pictured something of God's dealings with the nation Israel throughout the centuries. The vineyard of the Lord of Hosts was His people ; He hedged it round, and tilled the ground, and then let it out to husbandmen, the rulers and kings, and those who had authority over His people, and who were to care for them. And from time to time He sent His prophets, His messengers to look for fruit ; but the people who had been so richly blessed stoned one, and killed another, and maltreated another, until at last He said, " I have one Son ; I will send Him ; it may be that they will reverence Him when they see Him." They had been looking forward to the coming of the Messiah through the years, and you would have thought that they would have been so glad when He came. But no. He was not the One whom they had expected. They looked for a great warrior Messiah, who would deliver them from the Roman yoke. In the words of George Macdonald : " He came a little Baby thing that made a woman cry." And they did not recognise in the Babe of Bethlehem the promised Messiah. And when He grew up to manhood's estate, and went about doing good, and healing all who were oppressed of the devil, they did not see in Him the promised Saviour. So they said, " This is the heir ; come, let us kill Him, and the inheritance shall be ours." And they cast Him out of the vineyard. And the Lord Jesus turned to the Pharisees who had gathered about Him, and He said, " What do you think the Lord of the vineyard will do to those wicked husbandmen ? " And, taken un-awares, and not realising for the moment the full import of the parable, they said, " He will miserably destroy them ; and he will let out his vineyard to other husbandmen, which shall render him the fruits in their season." " Jesus saith unto them, Did ye never read in the Scriptures, The stone which the builders rejected, the same is become the head of the corner; this is the Lord's doing, and it is marvellous in our eyes." You go back to that Psalm, and there you have portrayed the Saviour coming into Jerusalem, and the people crying " Hosanna " to the King that cometh in the name of the Lord; and almost immediately following, there is the stone that the builders rejected. The people were familiar with that Scripture; it was a favourite Scripture among the Rabbis. They had a legend attached to it which may, or may not have been true. They said that that verse referred to a stone in connection with the building of Solomon's Temple. You remember that temple was built on the top of Mount Moriah; and in order to make a level platform it was necessary that great stones should be brought up from below, and placed in order upon the mount; and those stones were quarried out of the caverns below Jerusalem and all prepared for the building of the temple; and that temple went up silently. There was no sound of a hammer. It was God's picture of His present glorious temple, the temple not made with hands, the temple composed of living stones in which He Himself dwells.

" View the vast building, see it rise,
   The work how great, the plan how wise !
   Nor can that place be overthrown
   That rests upon the living stone."

So the temple was built of stones cut, and shaped,
and brought up to the top of the mount, rolled
over and lifted up into their place. It is said by
the Jews that as those stones came up from below
there was one for which the workman could find
no place ; it was different from the rest ; so
different that they could not see that there was
any place for it, and after a good deal of question-
ing they said, ' It is only in the way ; we had
better get it out of the way,' and so they rolled
it over the edge of the cliff and down into the
valley below. Years went by. Solomon was
many years building the temple ; the men
worked in relays six months at a time, and there
were very few working in the later years who
were there in the beginning ; and the time came
for the chief corner-stone to be fitted in its place,
and a message was sent, " Send us the chief
corner-stone," and the reply came back, " It was
sent up long ago ; and you have it there at the
top of the mount." " It is not here," they said.
" Well, we sent it up," came the reply. But
they could not find it. And an old workman who
had been with one of the early relays said, " I

remember now; there was a stone, now I come to think of it; it was different to the rest, and I believe it was the stone which would just have fitted in there as the chief corner-stone. We did not realise it at the time, and we threw it over the cliff, and it must be there still; we did not understand what we were doing." So they went down, and there in the valley, covered by debris, they found the rejected stone; and with a great deal of difficulty they hoisted it up again to the top of the rock, and fitted it into its place. The stone that the builders rejected had become the head of the corner. Jesus said, " Did ye never read that?" and He applied it directly to Himself. He was looking on to the Cross; He was the rejected stone. He foresaw Pilate's judgment hall as the people cried, " Away with Him; crucify Him." And the words of Pilate, " Shall I crucify your King?" and their cry, " We have no king but Caesar." They rejected the One whom God had sent; they rejected the promised Saviour; they rejected their Messiah. They did not understand. The apostle Peter said, " I know, brethren, that through ignorance ye did it." Even Pilate, as the agent of the Gentiles, did not understand, for the apostle Paul says, " that the prince of this world has blinded their eyes." They rejected Him when He came in lowly guise

as the sinner's Saviour. But he came, too, as the
King. He said, " The Kingdom of God is
among you." But they did not recognise the
King, and they refused Him ; and He said, " The
Kingdom of God shall be taken from you and
given to a nation bringing forth the fruits there-
of," a regenerated nation, a people who had been
born again of the Spirit of God, and who would,
therefore, value the Lord Jesus Christ.

The Saviour refers to two other Old Testament
scriptures. He says, " Whosoever shall fall on this
stone shall be broken ; but on whomsoever it
shall fall, it will grind him to powder." We have
a reference to this stone in Isaiah viii where, long
before, the prophet said in verse 13 : " Sanctify
the Lord of hosts himself ; and let him be your
fear, and let him be your dread. And He shall
be for a sanctuary ; but for a stone of stumbling
and for a rock of offence, for a gin and for a
snare to the inhabitants of Jerusalem. And
many among them shall stumble, and fall, and be
broken, and be snared, and be taken." This
prophecy was just about to be fulfilled. Every
word that God has written will have its fulfilment. He is the stone of salvation ; He is the
One that God sent but because of unbelief, and
because of eyes blinded by sin, instead of bringing salvation to Israel, He became a stumbling-

stone. And He says, " Whosoever shall fall upon this stone shall be broken." They rejected Him ; they fell over the stumbling-stone, and they have been broken. Oh, how they have suffered through years ! Our hearts are rightfully pained as we think of their present suffering. And as we look back over the centuries, has ever a people suffered as they have suffered ? No wonder Jeremiah, speaking for the nation, could say, " Is it nothing to you all ye who pass by ? Behold, and see if there be any sorrow like unto my sorrow, which is done unto me, wherewith the Lord hath afflicted me in the day of His fierce anger." We may rightly apply those words to the Blessed Saviour, remembering that He stood in Israel's place, and bore for every believer the judgments of God upon the Cross. But if you take them in their full context they refer to Israel after the flesh, God's earthly people. They fell over the stumbling-block, and they were broken to pieces. That explains their history through the years. That explains why everything is out of joint among the nations. If they had only received Him, and recognised in Him their rightful King, how different things would have been ! The angels sang at His birth, " Glory to God in the highest, and on earth peace, goodwill towards men." But nineteen hundred years have gone by, and there is no real, lasting peace yet; and He knew that it would be so, for He said, "Think not that I am come to send peace on earth; I came not to send peace, but a sword." The Prince of Peace was rejected, and all the warfare, and all the trouble, and all the sorrow that Israel and the nations have gone through during the past nineteen centuries have been the result of the rejection of the Lord Jesus Christ.

A number of years ago, out in San Francisco, we had that princely man of God, Henry Varley, holding a series of meetings, and I always feel that the two months I spent in intimate association with him when he was with us were my theological seminary. I had been preaching as a young man. I put in six and a half years as a Salvation Army officer, and then preaching as an evangelist for a year after that, but there was very much I needed to know. Henry Varley was very kind and fatherly, and he took me in tow. He always called me "Cromwell" because my name was "Ironside." He was such a fatherly man, and we had a delightful season together. During the time of his great meetings in what we called the Metropolitan Temple, a building seating over three thousand people, and which was filled night after night for a month, it was my privilege to have charge of the open-air work, and of the ushers. We used to have eight open-air meetings every night. One would begin about a mile away from the hall, another one two or three squares further up, and so on, and so on, and the last one right outside the Temple. When the time came it was my duty to go down to the most distant meeting and make the announcement concerning the large inside gathering, and then, singing a Gospel song, we would march up to the next meeting, make the announcement there, and pick them up, and then go on to the next, and do the same thing there. And by the time we reached the Temple there would be about four to five hundred of us in the procession. One night, I remember it so well, we had come to the last open-air meeting, we had made the announcement, and had urged the people to come into the Temple and hear God's servant. And just as we were turning away a fussy little man put down a box, and got on it, and said, " My friends, if you will wait a minute I have got something worth while to talk about. You have been listening to these religious fanatics who have been trying to tell you about the way of salvation, the way by which you may get into some mythical heaven after death. I will show you how we may make a heaven of this world. You do not need heaven after death ; you want heaven down here.

These religious people are just the agents of the capitalists; they keep you out of what is due to you; you must save yourselves." A lot of people stood and listened, and I said to our crowd, " You go on in, and I will stay outside here, and get the benefit of what this man is saying." He repeated a miserable bit of doggerel; you could not call it poetry; even the title was not grammatical. " They tells us there's a God; why don't He lend a hand ? " He repeated verse after verse describing the dreadful conditions prevailing in various parts of the world, winding up each verse with the refrain, " They tells us there's a God; why don't He lend a hand ? " The verses were truly pathetic; one verse described two little children trapped in a burning building crying for help, but no help came, and they were burned to death. Another verse described men in battle killing one another, for no real reason. And again there came the question, " They tells us there's a God; why don't He lend a hand ? " When he had finished, and had stepped down from his box, I said to him, " Are you sure of that ? " " Yes, I am," he replied. " Will you lend me your box ? " " All right," he said, and I got up on his box, and the crowd was a large one by now. I said, " My dear friends, if I can I want to try and answer the questions of this infidel to-night, ' They tells us there's a God; why don't He lend a hand ? ' We have an answer to that question in the Bible. God looked down on the earth, and He saw the misery and wretchedness of mankind, and all that sin had wrought. It is all the fruit of sin. War is the fruit of sin. Sickness, and disease, and death, are all the fruit of sin. He saw all the wretchedness that man was enduring, and His great heart was moved, and He said, I am going to lend a hand. I am going to do something for wretched humanity. I will send My Son. That is what He did. He sent the Lord Jesus Christ into the world, His only Son." I said to those standing around, " What are you doing to-night with the One whom God sent to lend a hand ? What did Israel do with Him ? What have the Gentiles done with Him, the anointed One of God, Jesus of Nazareth, who went about doing good, and healing all who were oppressed with the Devil ? Those blessed hands of His were always raised in mercy, and in loving kindness; and yet men deliberately rejected Him, and cried out, " Away with Him; crucify Him." That is what the world did with the One whom God sent to lend a hand. You might have thought that God's patience would have given out, and that He would have said, If that is the way they treat my Son, I will destroy them even as I destroyed the world by a Flood before. But no, instead God said, They have done their worst work; they can do nothing worse; and I am going to "make His soul an offering for sin," and through His infinite sacrifice I will proclaim redemption to every poor sinner in all the world who will trust Him as Saviour. After He died, God raised Him from the dead, and the Risen Christ ascended, and now His servants go forward everywhere preaching the Gospel of His grace to a needy world. And, my friends, because of the rejection of the Man whom God sent to lend a hand, there is still cruel warfare, there is still famine and sickness and disease and poverty and wretchedness in this world. And it is all because men refused the One whom God sent to lend a hand. But wherever men receive Him there is peace, there is joy, there is gladness, and everything around is changed. It is not simply that there is a preparation for heaven after death, but things are changed right here on earth. When men receive Him their lives are changed; their homes are changed; whole countries are changed; whole continents are changed when the Gospel is carried into them, and the message of Christ is made known to the men and women living there." "Now," I said to this man, "before you dare to stand up again and in your sneering way ask, "They tells us there's a God; why don't He lend a hand?" you settle in your own heart what you are going to do with the One whom God sent to lend a hand. What is your attitude going to be toward Him to-night? If you repent, He will save you, and He will forgive all your blasphemies, and all your hatred of His Name, and all the evil you have done. Kiss the Son lest He be angry, and you perish from the way." I do not know how he felt, but he turned and walked away, and a great crowd came thronging in to hear Henry Varley preach that night. Yes, Christ came down from Heaven's glory to Calvary's path of woe, and there He died — the rejected King, but the glorious Saviour.

Christ died for sinners, but because of their rejection, Israel, as a people, have been broken to pieces. If they had only understood; if they had only turned to God and sought His face as a nation how different things would have been!

But the Lord Jesus not only refers to that passage, He refers to yet another passage in Daniel ii. "But on whomsoever it shall fall, it will grind him to powder." That refers to His Second Coming when He shall be "revealed from heaven in flaming fire, with His holy angels, taking vengeance on them that know not God, and obey not the Gospel." The reference clearly is to Nebuchadnezzar's vision of the great metallic image representing the times of the Gentiles, with its head of gold, its breast and arms of silver, its thighs of brass, its legs of iron, its feet part of iron and part of clay. We are living in the days of the iron and clay. What means this struggle to-day between Fascism on the one hand, and Sovietism on the other? What means this clash between Capital and Labour, between Despotism and Social Democracy? The great question is, Which shall dominate the world? Which shall dominate the nations that come out of that old Roman Empire? We can almost see the ten kingdoms federation forming at the present time, which some day will be banded together as one. You say, We already have ten kingdoms. But Daniel is speaking of ten kingdoms which will be on the earth at one time, and all under the direction of one head, as the ten toes and feet of a man are under the control of the one head. The same thing is pictured in the Book of the Revelation, in the thirteenth chapter, when the ten kings give their power and authority to the Beast. And we can see everything working up to that. I do not believe that it will take place while the Church of God is on the earth. But the fact that things are so rapidly moving helps us to realise that we will not be here much longer. We will soon hear the voice of God and the sound of the trump that shall summon us to meet the Lord in the air. Meantime men are making a last effort to bring about a lasting peace and understanding among the nations. But while the Christ of God is still rejected, of course it will end in failure, as all man's pacts end in failure while Christ is ignored. Daniel says, " In the days of these things shall the God of heaven set up a kingdom that shall never be destroyed . . . The stone was cut out of the mountain without hands, fell on the feet of the image and it brake in pieces the iron, the brass, the clay, the silver, and the gold." All were destroyed and became the dust on the summer threshing-floor and the wind carried it away, and it was gone. Jesus Himself is the stone. God raised Him from the dead, and made Him the head-stone of the corner; and Israel was broken in pieces because they stumbled over Him. Some day He is coming again, and then it will be the Gentile powers that will be destroyed, and then " the kingdoms of this world will become the kingdoms of our God, and of His Christ."

So I think in this wonderful parable our Blessed Lord has given us a marvellous outline of what has taken place, and of what will take place when He comes back again in glory.

I wonder if we are all ready to meet Him. I wonder if everyone here has been washed from their sins in His precious blood. Listen : no one will be ready to meet the Lord when He comes the second time unless they have taken advantage of of what He did when He was here the first time. "For as it is appointed unto men once to die, and after this the Judgment, so Christ was once offered to bear the sin of many ; and unto them that look for Him shall He appear the second time, apart from the sin question." If you have not yet availed yourself of what He did when He was here before, I would plead with you do not seek your slumber to-night until you have bowed yourself at His feet, and told Him that you repent of the sin of having rejected Him for so long, that at last you are ready to receive Him, and to trust Him, and to accept Him as your own personal Saviour. And "to as many as received Him to them gave He the power to become the children of God, even to them that believe on His Name."

II

THE HOPE OF ISRAEL

" Let all the nations be gathered together, and let the people be assembled ; who among them can declare this, and shew us former things ? Let them bring forth their witnesses, that they may be justified ; or let them hear, and say, It is truth.

" Ye are My witnesses, saith the Lord, and My servant whom I have chosen ; that ye may know and believe Me, and understand that I am He ; before Me there was no God formed, neither shall there be after Me.

" I, even I, am the Lord ; and beside Me there is no Saviour " (Isa. xliii. 9–11).

" This people have I formed for Myself ; they shall shew forth My praise " (verse 21).

AGAIN in the forty-fourth chapter we hear God addressing His people the Jews, the nation of Israel, the sons of Jacob : " Ye are My witnesses." That is a very remarkable statement. The nation of Israel is distinctly designated by God as a testimony for Himself in the earth. In these first nine chapters of the last part of the prophecy of Isaiah, beginning with chapter xl, over and over again God challenges the representatives of every false religious system under heaven to prove that they are really divinely-inspired by telling of things to come. He says, If you can do that, then you deserve to be accredited ; but if you cannot do that, then listen, and I will do it. And so he opens up the future in a way that no uninspired man could possibly do, and it is in that connection that he speaks of the Children of Israel as His witnesses.

Let me say here that I do not make the distinction that some people make between the Jews and Israel. I have seen statements made that the Jews crucified Christ, but the Children of Israel did not. But my Bible says, " Ye men of the stock of Israel," and the apostle Peter drives home to them the fact that they crucified the Lord of glory. And so it is one people. The Lord Jesus Christ came to the lost sheep of the House of Israel, but they rejected Him, and for the present they are wanderers among the nations. " Blindness in part has happened unto Israel until the fulness of the Gentiles be come in." And it is to Israel that God is speaking. He calls them Israel, the sons of Jacob, when He says, " Ye are My witnesses." That does not exactly mean that they are witnesses because of their faithfulness to the Lord, but it means this ; that whether they are in the land, or out of the land, whether they are obedient to the Word of

God, or disobedient, whether they are enjoying His loving favour, or whether His hand is resting upon them in judgment, this nation proves that this Blessed Book is the inspired Word of God, because their history was foretold 3,500 years ago, and all down through the centuries it has been recorded by God's servants. It is a very remarkable thing, but this little Book with about a thousand pages, and which I can hold so conveniently in my hand, is absolutely the only book of prophecy in all the world. I remember that was impressed upon me when I was a very young Christian. I had only been converted a few months, and I went to hear a man who was announced to give a lecture on the Bible. It was quite a misleading announcement. I thought I was to hear someone who would open up the Scriptures to me ; but instead of that it turned out to be a lecture given by a man who was opposed to the Bible, an unbeliever. As I listened to him, as he brought up all the stock arguments against the inspiration of the Bible that so many gullible people have accepted through the years, I could not help feeling that any ordinarily instructed Sunday School scholar would have been able to answer them all. Then he came to one point that did floor me for a moment. Holding up the Bible, he said, " I have no doubt that some of you believe this Book to be the Word of God. But do you know why you believe it ? You believe it because your parents have told you it was God's Word. If you had been brought up in a Mohammedan home you would have believed that the Koran was the Word of God. If you had been brought up in a Buddhist home you would have accepted the Buddhist Scriptures as the Word of God. If you had been brought up in a Hindu home you would have accepted the Vedas as the Word of God." And, do you know, just for the moment that floored me. I had been brought up in a Christian home, and I had been taught all my life that the Bible is the Word of God, and I had to ask myself if that was the only reason I believed it. I was so troubled about it that I could hardly sleep that night. The next day I went to the Public Library, and I said to the lady there, " I would like to see all the different Bibles of the world." She said, " My dear boy, you know there is only one Bible." (She was a wise woman.) I said, " What I mean is this, I want the books that other nations accept in the place of our Bible." " Oh, I see," she said, " you want the sacred literature." So she led me to a ten-foot shelf where were translations put up in thirty-eight volumes of the sacred books of the

East. "That is what I want," I said. "I want to read them all." "You aren't going to take them all with you to-day, are you?" she asked. I said, "I have got three tickets, one in my mother's name, one in my brother's name, and one in my own name. I would like three of them." I took them away, and I read three that week; the next Saturday I got out three more, and I got going with those; and at last I had read through the whole set. Although I did not get a degree as Doctor of Comparative Religions, I certainly had studied them, and I have always been glad that I did, because I made some really interesting discoveries. In the first place, I had always believed that pagan religions had nothing but evil in them, but I found a lot of beautiful gems of truth in those different books, some very lovely things, I grant you, written in the most wretched connections. Some of the things there were so vile that if you had taken them out separately, and put them in an envelope and sent them through the post, and they had been discovered, you would have been arrested for sending obscene matter through the post. On the other hand, there were some beautiful gems of thought. However, when I had gone all through those thirty-eight volumes I realised that I had not found in them all one religious or moral truth that I did not have already in this little Book. That is a most marvellous thing. You could have sunk all those books to the bottom of the sea, and the world would not have lost one thing worth keeping if we still had the Bible. The next thing I found out was this, that there was nothing in any of those books to show a poor sinner how he might be delivered from sin, and how he might become a new creature. And the third thing I realised, and which has remained with me through the years, was, that in all those volumes there was not one solitary prophecy that had ever been fulfilled, or that was ever likely to be fulfilled. But how different with this Book! Here I find all the treasure and wisdom of God; here I learn how a poor, guilty sinner may be washed from his sins, and become a new creature in Christ Jesus; here I can trace out the future in a most marvellous way, for God Himself has spoken in His Word. And God has left in the world one particular nation as His own witness, as a testimony to the truth of this Book—the nation of Israel. Is it not remarkable that Moses, standing there in the plains of Moab 3,500 years ago, could foretell through the centuries, in the way he has done, the history of the Children of Israel. It is a most amazing thing. He told how they would enter into the Land, and how, as long as they walked in obedience to the will of God, they would have His blessing and His Fatherly care, and that He would take disease away from them, and they would prosper, and no enemy would be able to triumph over them. But, on the other hand, he foretold their apostacy, and their sin, and the judgment that would come upon them. He spoke of their going down to Babylon (though he did not use the actual name) and their return again when they called upon God. And he spoke of those greater judgments yet to come, when nations should come from afar, from the ends of the earth, like eagles flying. That prophecy had no reference to Babylon; Babylon was not afar off, Babylon was practically their next-door neighbour. But in the days that Moses spoke Italy was at the very ends of the earth, and the city of Rome was just a little mud village on the banks of the Tiber. And no one who had not been inspired by God could have ever dreamed that some day it would dominate the whole world, and the nation of Israel would be subject to that power. Moses said that they would come from the ends of the earth, and they would come as the eagle; and the eagle was the Roman insignia. And when the children of Israel saw the Roman eagle set up by the walls of Jerusalem they knew that the judgment predicted so long ago was about to fall. Moses described the march of the Romans down through the land, just as if he could see them, city after city falling before them, their orchards and vineyards destroyed, and the people smitten in such a way that thousands of them were slain, and the rest suffered so sorely because of famine and poverty that the awful vice even of cannibalism gripped them, and they ate their own children. It is all predicted there, and it had a terrible fulfilment seventy years after the birth of our Lord Jesus Christ. And when He came into this world, and He stood one day on the Mount of Olives looking down over Jerusalem, He foresaw all that Moses had predicted, and more, as He contemplated the sufferings of His people. For do not forget it, though Hitler may say He was not a Jew, He came into this world through a Jewish Mother, and He was subject to the laws of God as known only by Israel during all the years that He was here on earth. And as He stood there on the Mount of Olives, and looked forward, and saw what His people would pass through, we read that He wept over the city of Jerusalem, and over the people, because they " knew not the time of their visitation." And God's Word has been fulfilled to the letter; the people of Israel have been scattered everywhere. Just think of the utter temerity of Moses in making that prediction. You might say, Well he knew that he would be out of the way before the time could come, and before they could check him on it. But we know that the predictions he made have been fulfilled to the very letter. Suppose he had made the same predictions concerning the children of the half-brother that he made concerning the Children of Israel. Ishmael was the father of a great nation. Twelve tribes came from him just as eventually twelve tribes sprang out of Isaac through Jacob. There were twelve tribes of which Ishmael was the father. And suppose Moses had said that the sons of Ishmael, because of their sins—and they were as great sinners as the Jews—should be scattered among the nations, that everywhere in the world they would wander because of their transgression—why, the centuries since would have attested the falsity of such a prediction. More than 3,500 years have elapsed, and the children of Ishmael live to-day where they lived in the days of Moses. They have not been scattered all over the world. They are still there. You never see an Arab unless he comes round as a merchant through the country selling oriental stuff (probably made in Japan). You do

not run across many Arabs; they are still in
Arabia, and in the contiguous territory; while
the Jews have been scattered everywhere.   Suppose Moses had made the blunder of predicting
the same things concerning the sons of Edom
that he predicted concerning the sons of his twin
brother, Jacob, what a false prophet he would
have proved to be; because if he had said that
the Edomites would have been scattered throughout the world, centuries since would have proved
him to have been wrong.   You do not know
what an Edomite looks like because another
prophecy in this great Book says that God would
utterly blot Edom out from under Heaven.
You can go over the cities of Edom to-day; you
can walk through those cities, and into those
stone houses, and you can see the frescoes on
the walls as fresh as they were 1,600 years ago
when in some mysterious way the nation of
Edom was blotted out from under Heaven.
God's Word has been fulfilled to the very letter.
No, Moses was not guessing; he was speaking
by divine inspiration.   And so our Lord Jesus
Christ speaks of the judgment that is to come
upon the people because "they knew not the
time of their visitation."   He had come in fulfilment of the prophetic word.   In the beginning
the prophecy was given to our first parents in

the curse pronounced upon Satan : " The seed of the woman shall bruise the serpent's head." Now that is a remarkable expression. If anyone questions the Virgin Birth of our Lord Jesus Christ let him try and explain that. Every other human being that has ever come into the world has come through the seed of the man. But in that prophecy we read that it is the seed of the woman that was to bruise the serpent's head. Our Blessed Lord was to come into his world in a way that no one else had ever come.

Then you go on down through the years and you see God calling out Abraham. He says to Abraham, " In thee, and in thy seed, shall all the nations of the earth be blessed." Let us not forget that the promise made to Abraham abides to-day. God says, " I will bless them that bless thee, and curse him that curseth thee." One reason why I am absolutely certain that that gentleman over in Germany will never be able to carry out his plan in regard to the Jews is this, that he is already under the divine curse because of his actions towards the seed of Abraham. And that is true not only of his natural seed, but of those who have become his spiritual seed because they have the same faith that dwelt in Abraham.

And there was the promise also made to David; the promised seed was to come through him. David's Son is to sit eventually upon his throne. And so the people waited, and the time for the fulfilment of the promise drew nigh, and Jesus came, but when He came they did not recognise Him, and they rejected Him. They said, " This is the heir ; come, let us kill him, and the inheritance shall be ours." In Pilate's judgment hall they rejected Him, and desired that a murderer should be granted unto them. Oh, how much they have suffered since ! It has often been my privilege to preach the Gospel to Jewish audiences ; and there is one question that I always like to put to the individual Jew when he comes to talk to me afterwards, and it is this : " What is the greatest sin that a Jew can possibly be guilty of ? " and they invariably answer in the same way, " The sin of idolatry." I say, " How do you know that is the greatest sin ? " and they reply, " Because our Bible often warns us against that sin ; and when our fathers forgot the Word of God, and began to worship idols, the hand of God was against them." God would not protect them against their enemies, and the time came when they were carried down to Babylon, and He would not allow them to return to their land until they had repented. They were seventy years in Babylon; and they have never been idolators since. The evil spirit of idolatry was cast out of them; and they returned to their land, and they were like a house empty, swept and garnished, but with nothing in it to take the place of the old idolatrous spirit.

And then I say to them, "Now I want to ask you another question. How long have you been out of your land?" They reply, "Approximately nineteen hundred years." "And what sin did your fathers commit?" I ask, "And what sin are you still committing, by reason of which you have been driven out of your land, and have been kept out of it for nineteen hundred years?" That is a solemn question for an honest Jew to attempt to answer. It is because of his rejection of the promised Messiah when He came. That is the only adequate explanation of all Israel's sufferings through the years. You say, Oh, well, it is perfectly right to make them suffer. No, No! God said to Edom, "When I was disciplining My people you stood by and looked on, and mocked at their sorrows. You should not have done that. I have been dealing with them, now I shall have to deal with you." We, as Christian people, should surely remember that the heart of our Lord Jesus Christ is concerned about His nation still.

I remember some years ago I was in the city of Detroit holding some meetings there; I was staying away out in the suburbs, and one day I was about to go into town, and I had to walk in order to reach the tram car, and just as I reached the street on which it ran the rain began to fall. I said to myself, I had better hurry back for my umbrella—and then I remembered that my umbrella had a broken rib, but I decided that at least I could get my coat to keep me from getting too wet. I was hurrying back to the house when, providentially, as it seemed, an old Russian Jew came round the corner. He was one of those orthodox Jews with the big curls. He had under his arm a bundle of umbrellas. I said to him, "You are just the man I want. Do you mind walking along to the house with me, and fixing an umbrella for me." He said, "I will gladly come." So he came along, and he sat in the porch doing the work. There he sat with his seamed face, and those deep-set eyes that spoke of terrible suffering, and my heart went out to him; and I was praying that God would help me in some way to give my testimony. Finally the job was done. "How much do I owe you?" I asked. He told me it was 35 cents, that is about 1*s*. 6*d*. I said, "That's not very much; if that is all you get for a single job you must have rather a hard time." "It is very hard, but that is all the job is worth," he replied. I said, " I am going to pay you what you have asked me, but I want you also to accept this 50 cents, this 2*s*., just as a gift to help you along a little, and I give it to you in the name of Jesus Christ." I dropped it into his hand, and he almost let it slip through his fingers, but he was too good a Jew for that, he did not let it through, actually, but held on to it. He looked at me, and then at the money, and he said, " My God ! In the name of Jesus Christ they burned my house over my head. In the name of Jesus Christ they drove my wife and children out into the snow. In the name of Jesus Christ they robbed me of everything that I had. I escaped from Russia, and I came over here to try to make another start. I have been here four years, and now, for the first time, somebody speaks to me of Jesus Christ, and in the name of Jesus Christ he gives me more money than I asked for. I cannot make it out." I said, " Sit down, and let me talk to you." I told him that no one who really loved the Lord Jesus Christ would be a persecutor of the Jew. I told him that Jesus loved His people, and how He said, " Inasmuch as ye have done it unto one of the least of these My brethren, ye have done it unto Me." I had an opportunity of

preaching the Gospel of the grace of God to
him. I do not know just how much went in.
I had to hurry off to catch the street car, and he
moved on, and I saw him walking down the
street with his hand shaking and his head bowed,
and though I could not hear him I knew he was
saying, " In the name of Jesus Christ he gives me
more money than I asked." And I prayed the
Lord that He would make that little coin the
means of bringing the Gospel to his poor troubled
heart. How much the professing Christian
Church will have to answer for some day for the
way it has misrepresented the Lord Jesus Christ to
the Jew ! Truly they are suffering sorely for
their sin, but we are not to add to their suffering,
we are to manifest towards them the grace of
our Lord Jesus.

The wonderful thing is this, that the same
Scriptures that declare that Israel will be scattered declare also that they will be re-gathered in
God's good time ; they are going back to their
own land. The Scriptures indicate two returns
to the Land : the return of a portion of the
people in unbelief, with their hearts still hardened
against Christ, their eyes still blinded, and still
without understanding as to the truth of the
Gospel ; and then after they are in the land there
will be the revelation of God's Son from Heaven,

and a nation will be born in a day, and then the
Word of God will go out to the ends of the earth,
and the entire redeemed nation will be restored
to God, and to their ancient home, and the Lord
Jesus will reign over them from the river to the
ends of the earth.   I believe the most striking
evidence that the coming of our Lord Jesus Christ
is drawing very near is the Return of the Jews,
even in their unbelief, to the Land of Palestine.
I have no question that God Himself was over-
ruling in the affairs of the nations when He permitted the World War, and when He brought it
to an end as soon as the British Government in
the Balfour Declaration opened up Palestine as a
home for the Jews.   And the troubles that have
come about since do not upset my confidence in
the least that God is working out His own plans.
Of course the difficulty is to get Isaac and Ishmael
together in the one country.   They could not
get along before, and they are not able to get
along now.   The marvellous thing is that when
the Lord Jesus comes the light of His favour is
going to rest upon the tents of Kedar as well as
upon the House of Israel.   The tents of Kedar
are the tents of the Arabs.   Some day the nation
that sprang from Ishmael will be brought into
the faith of Abraham as well as the nation that
sprang from Isaac.   When the Lord Jesus was

on the Mount of Olives, and He saw the coming
destruction of Jerusalem, and its glory passing
away, the disciples said to Him, "Master, when
shall these things be, and what shall be the sign
of Thy Coming, and of the end of the age?"
And answering both questions, Christ predicted
the destruction of the Temple, which took place
some forty years after His death, and resurrection
and ascension into Heaven, and then leaping over
the present dispensation, He carried the minds of
His disciples right on to the end of the age, and
of His Coming again.   And as an evidence of
His Coming, He said, "When ye see the fig-tree
putting forth her green leaves, then ye know that
summer is nigh.   So likewise when ye shall see
all these things, know that it is near, even at the
doors." Mark's Gospel puts it, "then know that
He is near." I have no question but that we are
living in the days of the budding of the fig-tree,
for the fig-tree is the recognised symbol of the
nation of Israel throughout the Word of God.
Take passage after passage that deals with this
question, and you will see that that statement is
true. So the Lord Jesus is really telling His people
that when they see great national movements in
Israel, when they see them again acting as a
people in the world, then they may know that
the Coming of the Lord is very close at hand.

I remember, when we were still in the throes of the World War, I was giving a series of Bible talks in the Y.W.C.A. Hall in San Francisco one night a week all through the autumn and winter. Most of the young ladies present had never known anything much about prophecy ; but they asked the Association Directress that they might study it, and she had applied to a good many different clergymen, but they had all refused to accept the invitation. "Fools rush in where angels fear to tread," and when they applied to me I expressed my delight at doing so. I had a class of about two hundred, and we moved on through the Book of Revelation chapter by chapter, and we had just reached chapter xi. And I remember very well that night I tried to point out that that chapter indicated the coming day when the people would go back to Palestine, and would re-build the Temple there in their own land. They were all greatly stirred. When the meeting was over I found that I had missed the ferry boat, and that there would not be another for an hour ; that gave me plenty of time to take a two-mile walk to the ferry. Presently I saw a lusty-lunged individual come tearing out of the San Francisco *Examiner* building with a big pile of papers, screaming at the top of his voice, "Allenby has taken Jerusalem." I said, "My boy, give me a paper. I have waited thirty years for that news." I shall never forget the thrill that came to my heart as I got on to the ferry boat, and settled down to read that stirring account of Allenby's entering into the holy city, without the firing of a single shot. I realised that we had moved on into the last epoch, in all probability, of the times of the Gentiles. And if you will allow me to put this in as a parenthesis. I do not know of any Scripture that tells us it was necessary that the Church should continue her testimony for this past twenty years. But I take it as an evidence of God's grace to a guilty world, that instead of closing up the dispensation twenty years ago He has kept the Gospel message sounding out, and thousands have been added to the Body of Christ. I think this last twenty years have been some of the greatest missionary years in all the history of the world. I believe that God is giving the last call to the Gentile nations in order that the Body of Christ may be completed before the Lord Jesus comes to receive His own.

I have been told by some ministers that this doctrine of the Lord's Coming is a very subversive doctrine, and that it is likely to upset the Churches. As one minister said, " It would cut the throat of Missions." Why, my dear friends, it is the very opposite. I have the honour, a quite undeserved one, of being minister of the Moody Memorial Church in Chicago. Now the Moody Church was founded on these precious truths. Eighty years ago Mr. Moody started a little Mission Sunday School that grew into the Moody Church of to-day, and this church has a membership of about 4,000 people, most of them poor, or in very ordinary circumstances. I do not think we have got a really rich man amongst us. Eight years ago some had a lot of paper securities stored away, but to-day most of it is good for nothing. These men's fortunes have been swept away, and many of them are now in very difficult circumstances. Let me tell you this, that that church has 108 foreign missionaries, out of our own membership and out of that number we support outright seventy-two of them, and we contribute what we can to the rest. Which means that every year we gather together for Missions in Chicago something like £10,000, besides all that has to be raised to carry on the local work at home. If you were to ask our people what it was that stirred them to give like that in support of missionary work they would tell you, " It is because we believe in the near Return of our Lord Jesus Christ, and that we want to get as many people to meet Him before He comes as we possibly can." Yes, the solution of Israel's problems will be the Coming again of our Lord Jesus Christ. And oh, thank God, soon He will appear; after they have passed through the trials of the Great Tribulation, the time of Jacob's trouble, they are going to see Him, when He returns and when His feet shall stand upon the Mount of Olives. I stood on the Mount of Olives three years ago, and I wondered just where He would stand when He comes. There was a big earthquake there shortly before, and scientists went out to investigate, and they sent back word that there was a geographical fault running through the mountains of Lebanon. Some day, they said, there will be another great earthquake, and it may split the Mount of Olives in two. I know what will make that mountain split in two. It will be when His blessed feet touch that mount from which He ascended to the glory; then it will part asunder, and the various things predicted in the Book of Zechariah will all be fulfilled, and Israel " shall look on Him whom they have pierced, and they shall mourn for Him as one that mourneth for His own son, and shall be in bitterness for Him, as one that is in bitterness for his first-born." " In that day there shall be a fountain opened to the house of David, and to

the inhabitants of Jerusalem for sin and for un-
cleanness." People generally misquote that passage. They say " a fountain shall be opened *in*
the house of David." The Scripture says " a
fountain shall be opened *to* the house of David."
If in that day the nation as such will turn to the
Lord, they will be one people in the land recognising their Messiah, and enjoying His loving
favour throughout the glorious Kingdom Age.

Now what about any of you who are here to-
night, and who are not saved, whether Jew or
Gentile? What you need is to know Christ for
yourself before that day comes, for if that day
comes, and you are still in your sins, you will be
left on the wrong side of the shut door, like
those foolish virgins who came knocking only to
hear Him say, " I know you not." If you have
never trusted the Saviour for yourself, turn to
Him before you sleep ; own your guilt, and trust
His grace, that you, too, may with gladness wait
for the coming of God's Son from Heaven.

III

THE HOPE OF THE NATIONS

Haggai ii. 6–9
Hebrews xii. 25–29

LAST evening I was trying to speak to you on the
Hope of Israel, on God's promises to Israel, and
the way in which He is eventually going to carry
them out.

I am thinking more to-night of the many
prophecies of Scripture that have to do with the
nations of the world, and the blessing that is
promised to the Gentile peoples in the end time.
You notice this expression in the seventh verse
of the second chapter of Haggai, that God is
going to shake the nations, and then, he says,
after the shaking of the nations " the desire of all
nations shall come." I suppose we might think
of that expression in two ways. We might
think of the desirable One ; and that, of course,
is the Lord Jesus Christ. For there can be no
real lasting peace or blessing for the nations of the
world until the Coming again of the Lord Jesus
Christ, when He shall be owned as King of

kings, and Lord of lords. Then, too, we might think of that expression as referring to the desirable things of all nations. What are the things that the nations desire ? What are the desirable things ? Well, we think of lasting peace, of prosperity, of health for the people of the nations, we think of happiness and joy. All of those things the nations are seeking after, and yet how dreadfully they have failed in the attainment of them. But some day the desirable things of all nations will come. The Old Testament bears witness to this, and the New Testament confirms it. All through the writings of the prophets we have the Spirit of God pointing us on to a time of fullness of blessing for this earth, when righteousness will cover the earth as the waters cover the sea, when men shall learn war no more, when they shall beat their swords into plough-shares, and their spears into pruning-hooks. We certainly have not reached that time yet ; in fact, we are experiencing the very opposite. Now we are gathering up all the scrap iron we can find in order to turn it into a means of destruction. But in that day which is coming the instruments of destruction will be turned into instruments for the blessing of mankind. The New Testament takes up the story, and carries our minds on to the time when the

Kingdom of God will be set up all over this earth. In the Book of the Revelation we read of a time when the kingdoms of this world shall become the kingdoms of our God and of His Christ. This is the goal to which everything is moving on. Yet I am sure we have to confess that at present, if we judge by the things we see, there does not seem to be much prospect of a very speedy realisation of these dreams. For over nineteen hundred years have gone since the Lord Jesus Christ came into this scene, and since the angels sang at His birth, " Glory to God in the highest, and on earth peace, goodwill towards men." In spite of all our boasted civilization the world to-day is just a great armed camp ; we seem no nearer to universal peace and blessedness than we were when the Saviour came.

Then, again, think of the question of world conversion. Scripture clearly indicates that the day will come when all the nations of the earth will own the authority of the Lord Jesus Christ. But look at things to-day. For nineteen hundred years the Gospel of the grace of God has been proclaimed. Millions have been saved, we can thank God for that ; marvellous changes have taken place through the preaching of the Gospel ; and yet it is a solemn fact that there are far more heathen in the world to-night than there were when the Lord Jesus Christ gave that great commission to His disciples to go into all the world and to preach the Gospel to every creature. Recently, we have seen whole nations, where the Gospel has been proclaimed, repudiating the Gospel, and turning away from the Word of God ; even the very nation that God used to light the Reformation fires, in large measure, spurns the testimony of Holy Scripture, and seeks to throttle the preaching of the Gospel. When we think of what has taken place in Russia we might well pause and ask ourselves, Is it possible that the world will ever be converted through the preaching of the Gospel ? Undoubtedly our commission is to preach it everywhere, to proclaim its message to men in every land, and of every clime, to tell them that " this is a faithful saying, and worthy of all acceptation, that Christ Jesus came into the world to save sinners." But if we are dependent on the preaching of the Gospel to bring in this era of everlasting peace and righteousness, then it must be evident that it will be a long time ere that takes place.

What does Scripture really reveal in regard to this ? There are different ways of looking at the last things. There are three great outstanding schools in connection with the study of the prophetic Word, and all of them are linked with the word "Millennium." Sometimes we have heard it objected that we never get the word "Millennium" in our English Bible. That is perfectly true. But there are lots of other words that we do not get in our English Bible, and yet much as we love and cherish our Bible, we do not want to part with them. I have never found the word "Substitution" in my Bible, but I know that Christ took my place upon the Cross, and that He bore my sins on the tree. I have never found the word "Trinity" in my English Bible, but I know that God exists in three glorious Persons—Father, Son, and Holy Spirit. So I am not going to give up the words which stand for great truths simply because I do not find them in my English Bible. And so with the word "Millennium." Though I do not find the word "Millennium" there, I certainly find that which answers to it. For six times in the twentieth chapter of the Book of the Revelation we read of the thousand years. We read of the righteous dead who live and reign with Christ a thousand years. We read that "the rest of the dead lived not again until the thousand years were finished." We read that Satan is to be bound, and is not to be permitted to deceive the nations for a thousand years. And we read that when those thousand years are expired he shall be loosed out of his prison, and that after the thousand years the wicked dead will be raised and brought forth to judgment. Now it is certainly quibbling in the light of passages like these to deny the Scripturalness of the term " Millennium." The word is simply a quicker way of saying " a thousand years."

The three schools I referred to have to do with the " Millennium." There are those who tell us that the Millennium is simply another name for the glorious Kingdom of our Lord Jesus Christ; that His rule of righteousness over all the earth will be brought in by the preaching of the Gospel; that we are to preach the Word, that we are to go into all the world, and to gather in the lost, and, finally, when everyone has been converted, then the Millennium will be here, and our Blessed Lord will come at the end of it, and will wind everything up. That view is generally called Post-Millenniallism.

Then there are those who believe in the Coming again of the Lord Jesus Christ, but, somehow or another, they cannot believe that the Millennium will ever be brought in until Christ Himself appears. We believe (and I say " we " now, because I identify myself with this group) that the Coming of the glorious Kingdom of our

Lord Jesus Christ awaits the Return of the King.
We sang just now :

> " Our Lord is now rejected,
>   And by the world disowned.
> By the many still neglected,
> And by the few enthroned.
>   But soon He'll come in glory,
>   The hour is drawing nigh.
> For the crowning day is coming
>   By and by."

And because we believe that there will be no
Millennium until Christ comes first, we are
generally designated Pre-Millennialists.

Then there are some folk who drop the Millennium out altogether. I do not know how
they can do it consistently. You cannot read
your Bible intelligently unless you accept what it
teaches, that eventually the authority of the Lord
Jesus Christ is going to be established over all the
earth. But those who deny the Millennium altogether are known as A-Millennialists. My friend,
Dr. Pettingill, was with you recently. He tells
how a brother came to him one day and said,
" I am neither a pre-Millennialist, nor a post-
Millennialist. I do not know just how to desig-
nate myself." " Oh," said Dr. Pettingill, " there
need be no difficulty about that. You are a
pre-posterous Millennialist ! " I am afraid a
good many people would rightly deserve that

title. The Bible does teach the triumph of righteousness, an era of universal peace and blessing; it does teach the reign of the Lord Jesus Christ over all the earth. But the question is, Will that be brought in by the preaching of the Gospel as we are doing it at present, or does it await the Return of the Lord Jesus Christ from Heaven?

Now I want to try and lay down a few propositions that indicate the correctness of the latter view. I hope you will be a little patient with me if I seem to be rather slow about this, but I would like to make this clear, for I am not talking to old friends who come to all the prophetic meetings, and who know all the " ins and outs " of this thing. You can sit there, and listen to me, and you may say, " Well, dear me, our brother may be a bit earnest about this, but he has got a lot to learn ! " I thoroughly agree with you. I am not trying to teach you anything. I am rather thinking of folk to whom these things are somewhat new, who have never given much consideration to the prophetic teaching of the Word of God. And in order to try to help them I am going to lay down some propositions, which I think you will admit before I get through, are absolutely logical. I am going to try to put them in syllogistic form.

My first proposition is this : There can be no Millennium until the Second Coming of our Lord Jesus Christ. For there can be no Millennium till Satan is bound. That is the major premise. The minor premise is this : Satan is to be bound at the Second Coming of our Lord Jesus Christ. Therefore, there can be no Millennium until Satan is bound. Is not that logical? Think it through for a moment. It is perfectly clear in the twentieth chapter of the Book of the Revelation that the binding of Satan is that which introduces the Millennium. He is to be bound for a thousand years. But it is equally clear that the binding of Satan takes place immediately after the descent of our Blessed Lord from Heaven. In chapter xix you see Christ coming out of the skies, pictured as a warrior riding upon a white horse, and with the armies from Heaven following Him. And Satan is dealt with ; he is cast into the bottomless pit, and then the Millennium begins.

Now for the second proposition. There can be no Millennium until Christ comes, because there can be no Millenniuum ntil anti-christ is destroyed. But the anti-christ has to be destroyed at the Second Coming of our Lord Jesus Christ, and, consequently, there can be no Millennium until Christ comes. Is that right ? Is that logical—that there can be no Millennium until Christ comes because there can be no Millennium until anti-christ is destroyed? You cannot think of Christ and anti-christ reigning at the same time. Therefore anti-christ must be put out of the way before the Millennium begins. I do not care who you understand the anti-christ to be. You may accept the historical view, and believe the Pope represents the anti-christ. Very well, there will be no Pope in the Millennium. On the other hand, you may accept the view that Islam is the anti-christ. Very well, there will be no Mohammedanism in the Millennium. Or you may accept the view that some of us hold, that the anti-christ is to be a definite individual who is to be raised up in the last days, and who will sit in the temple of God showing himself that he is God, and the apostate part of the Jewish nation will accept him as their king and messiah. But he is to be destroyed before the Millennium Kingdom of our Lord Jesus Christ is set up. You may even accept the view of many Roman Catholics that the anti-christ simply represents some Protestant system. Well, whatever it is, it has to be destroyed before Christ comes, and before the Millennium takes place. Listen to the Scripture. After describing the anti-christ in 2 Thessalonians ii. the Apostle Paul says: "Whom the Lord shall consume with the spirit of his mouth, and shall destroy with the brightness of his coming." Therefore the anti-christ will be destroyed at the Second Coming of Christ. So that there can be no Millennium until after the Second Coming of Christ. If you know of any Scripture that contradicts it, then come and tell me. But I shall have been terribly misled if that is not in accordance with the Word of God.

My third proposition is this : There can be no Millennium until Christ comes because there can be no Millennium until all delegated Gentile power has been destroyed ; but the destruction of Gentile power is to take place at the Second Coming of Christ. Now is that not true ? Can you imagine Jesus reigning with Hitler, and Mussolini, and Stalin ? No ! All Gentile designated power must be destroyed before the kingdoms of this world can become the kingdoms of our God, and of His Christ. And that will only take place at the Lord's Return. Our Lord Jesus Himself, speaking of that stone of which Daniel tells us in his second chapter, says, " On whomsoever it shall fall, it will grind him to powder." That great image represents the Gentile powers set up in independence of God. God Himself designates the rulers ; He puts people into authority, and they go on in independence of Him. But the day is coming when the Lord

Jesus is going to return from Heaven, and the stone, cut out without hands, is to fall upon the feet of that great image, the Gentile powers, and the gold, and the silver, and the brass, and the iron and clay will be broken to pieces, and shall become like the dust of the threshing-floor, and the wind shall carry them away, and they shall be gone; and the stone shall become a great mountain filling the whole earth.

Then, again, there can be no Millennium till Christ comes because there can be no Millennium until the nation of Israel, the Jewish people, shall be restored to God, and restored to the land of their fathers. But the restoration of Israel to God awaits the Second Coming of the Lord Jesus Christ; and it is when He shall return that they will "look on Him whom they pierced, and shall mourn for Him, as one mourneth for his only son, and shall be in bitterness for him, as one that is in bitterness for his first-born." Then, again, there can be no Millennium till Christ comes because there can be no Millennium until the dead in Christ are resurrected. He has given them the promise that they are going to reign with Him in that glorious day. But the dead in Christ are to be resurrected at the Second Coming of the Lord Jesus Christ, and, therefore, there can be no Millennium until the Lord Jesus Christ returns again. Further, there can be no Millennium until Christ comes because there can be no Millennium until the living believers are changed, and caught up to be with the Lord. He has promised that they shall be changed, and that they shall come with Him in power and glory when He reigns over this earth. The living believers are to be changed, and caught up at the Return of Christ; and, therefore, there can be no Millennium until Christ comes.

Now you just work these propositions out for yourselves and see if I am correct. If I am not, then refuse them. And if they are in accordance with the Word of God, believe them, and search His Word to see what He has revealed concerning His glorious reign upon the earth.

Another thing we might well take into consideration is this. The Lord Jesus Christ has clearly taught us that when He comes back again He will not find a converted world. He says in one place, " As it was in the days of Noah so shall it be at the Coming of the Son of Man. They were eating and drinking, marrying and giving in marriage, until the day that Noah entered into the ark . . . so shall also the coming of the Son of man be." I need hardly say to you that the days of Noah were not the days of a converted world. They were days when corruption and violence filled the earth ; and out of that earth God took in sovereign grace a little group, and saved them in the ark through the Flood to bring in a new race after the destruction of the old one. And the Lord Jesus says, In the same way when I come again I will find corruption and violence filling the earth, but I will find my own little flock serving Me, and loving Me, and I will take them to be with Myself before judging the earth, and before I bring in My glorious Kingdom. In another place He is warning of conditions that will prevail, even among His own, and He puts the rather sad question, " When the Son of man cometh shall He find faith on the earth ? " If I were a good Post-Millennialist I should answer that question like this : " Why, Master, you certainly will. You will find us all converted, and waiting for you. You will find faith spread abroad everywhere." But the Lord indicates nothing of the kind. He pictures rather a faithful few, clinging to God, and His Word ; and the mass of people rejecting Him. The apostles take up the same story. The Apostle Paul indicates that that day shall not come except there come first the apostasy, and the revealing of the man of sin. And the other writers speak of the same thing. Paul says in another place that " evil men and seducers shall wax worse and worse, deceiving, and being deceived." That does not look like a Millennium before Christ comes. We may be sure of this, that all men's efforts to bring about universal peace and righteousness before the Coming again of our Lord Jesus Christ are destined to end in failure. Well, you say, this is very discouraging. What are we going to do? Just drop our hands, and say, " It's no use ; things are going from bad to worse ? " Nothing of the kind. We have our work to do. We have been commissioned to go to men with the glorious Gospel of Christ, and when men believe that Gospel they are changed within, for they are born again ; they become new creatures in Christ Jesus. The way to create a new society is by creating new creatures. He makes men different, and then their environment becomes different. People have an idea that if you can only change a man's environment you may make a saint of him. But it does not work. When General William Booth was in America telling us about his " Darkest England " plan, he described very carefully what he proposed to do for the poor and the needy. And he said, " My dear comrades, don't make the mistake of substituting the alleviation of social ills for the regeneration of men and women," and he used this graphic illustration : " Take a man out of the slums of London, a poor, ragged, drunken man, separated from his family, get him to sign the pledge, and take him off into the country; settle him in a new home; bring his wife and children back to him, and give them every comfort. Get him a position where he can earn enough to keep his family properly. And then let him die in his sins, and go to hell at last. Really I would not bother with it; it would not be worth while." I shall never forget the effect of his words. Our business is to make new men by preaching the Gospel of the grace of God. We gladly admit this, that wherever men believe the Gospel they want to do all they can to better the condition of their fellows, and of course they will be interested in peace among the nations; of course they will pray for kings and for those in authority that we may lead a quiet and peaceable life in all godliness. Of course they will be interested in every movement that makes for the betterment of society. On the other hand, they will always recognise that the ideal conditions toward which the nations are looking will never be brought about until the Lord Jesus Christ Himself comes back. God has not changed His plan because men do not fall in with it. Things will never be right in this world until the Coming of the Son of man to reign as King. You remember what it says in the second Psalm. "The kings of the earth set themselves, and the rulers take counsel together, against the Lord, and against his anointed, saying, Let us break their bands asunder, and cast away their cords from us." They said, We will not subject ourselves to Him. And so they refused the Kingdom in refusing the King. The Lord Jesus Christ came as King, and He said, "The Kingdom of God is among you." But they said, We have no king but Caesar ; and they rejected the true King, and they have been ruled by the world Caesars to their hurt ever since. They cried out, "His blood be upon us, and on our children." Oh, how truly that prayer has been answered through the centuries ! Though men rejected Him when He came to this earth, yet individually we may receive the King in faith, and may know what it is to enter in spirit into the blessedness of the Kingdom of God. We enter into the blessings of the Kingdom by an inward faith. The King Himself is not yet visibly manifested here on the earth. He is like the householder going into the far country to receive for himself a kingdom and to return ; and during His absence we are seeking to serve Him here, to work in His interests, and to bring as many men and women as possible to own His authority.

But going back to the second Psalm. The nations repudiated the King. Does that change God's plan? No. He says, "Yet have I set My King upon My holy hill of Zion." It is as though He says, "I have not changed my plan in the least. My King is going to reign from the river to the ends of the earth. He is going to have His throne on Mount Zion. My promise made to David is going to be fulfilled. He shall never want a man to sit upon His throne." Yes, the day will come when Christ shall reign over a redeemed universe. But, in the meantime, the invitation goes out to all men everywhere, "Kiss the Son, lest He be angry, and ye perish from the way."

I have heard people say sometimes, "Why, if I believed what you believe, that the world is not going to be converted by the preaching of the Gospel, that our national and international problems are not going to be solved, and that we have to wait for the Return of Christ, why, it would throttle all Christian effort, and I should be utterly discouraged about work for God." May I ask why? Recognising the fact that the world is in revolt against Christ, I can go to men as His ambassador beseeching them, in Christ's stead, that they be reconciled to Him. And I know that wherever men receive His Gospel, wherever they believe His Word, they are brought out from under the authority of darkness, and translated into the Kingdom of the Son of His love. But there is a difference between the Kingdom set up in the heart of the believer and the Kingdom set up over all the earth, an outward and visible Kingdom. The apostle John uses a very suggestive expression in the Book of the Revelation. He says, " I John, who also am your brother, and companion in tribulation, and in the kingdom and patience of Jesus Christ, was in the isle that is called Patmos, for the Word of God, and for the testimony of Jesus Christ." The King will come by and by, and those who are identified with Him now " in the kingdom and patience of Jesus Christ " will reign with Him eventually in the displayed Kingdom of God. But, in the meantime, we are to seek to do what we can to win poor sinners to Himself. If there are any here out of Christ, who have never yet bowed the knee in repentance at His feet, I plead with you, in view of His near Return, in view of the fact that soon the Lord Jesus Christ is coming back from Heaven to take His own people to be with Himself, I plead with you to come to Him even to-night ; come to Him with all your sin, and with all your guilt. Do not try to hide anything. You remember that prayer of David. He said, " O God, pardon my iniquity for it is great."

We might have thought he would have said, " O God, pardon my iniquity, for it is not very great ; I am not so very bad." That is the way some people seem to put it. But it is only a great God and a great Saviour who can deal with a great sin like mine. If you are ready to come to Him like that, knowing the blessedness of reconciliation to God here and now, then you will be numbered amongst those who are waiting for the Return of the Lord Jesus Christ, and the fulfilment of the promises that He has given us in His holy Word.

Sometimes some of my brethren who do not believe in the literal Millennium tell me that my view of things is a very carnal one, and they cannot understand how I can hold such worldly expectations of a literal Kingdom of Christ in this world. And yet how often I find that people who talk like that are devoting a greater part of their time in an endeavour to improve this world. People who talk in that way are often the folk who are far more concerned about little reform movements than they are about preaching the Gospel of the grace of God, and yet they do not seem to think that that is carnal. Why, we would all like to see poverty abolished ; we would all like to see the haunting fear of war driven away ; we would all like to see men and women everywhere enjoying good health and prosperity. It is not carnal to long for that. And this Blessed Book tells us that some day the desire of all nations shall come ; and God is not going to allow the affairs of this world to be wound up before He has given to mankind a perfect Kingdom for a thousand wonderful years, and He is going to manifest His power in the blessing of the world in just the way it longs for. I never listen to a wild-eyed Communist standing on a soap box ranting against the prevailing order, but I say to myself, " Poor fellow. What you really want is the Coming again of our Lord Jesus Christ, but you do not realise it." That is going to put everything right. We will have real Communism then. Why, then every man shall sit under his vine and under his fig-tree. All poverty will cease out of the land, and we will have ideal conditions, which Scripture describes as the days of heaven upon earth. Who would not long for a time like that ? Someone says, " You do not expect to be living here on the earth then." Perhaps not, but I shall do a lot of visiting here. My home is going to be in the new Jerusalem. I believe the children of God will bear about the same relationship to the saints in the Millennium that the angels bore to the patriarchs in the old dispensation. When God wanted to send a message to the patriarchs He sent angels. And I think that if God wanted to send a message down to London, He would say, "Here, Mr. Pitt, you used to be down there; you know them there; you go down there and carry this message for Me to them." And I hope I may have the privilege of slipping down to Chicago (if the gangsters have not wiped it out before then!). And simply because I am interested on the heavenly side, it does not mean that I am not interested in seeing the era of peace on the earth, and goodwill among men, and the coming in of the Kingdom of God in all its power and glory. Peter says, "We have not followed cunningly-devised fables, when we made known unto you the power and coming of our Lord Jesus Christ, but were eye-witnesses of His majesty." He says, "We have also a more sure word of prophecy whereunto ye do well that ye take heed, as unto a light that shineth in a dark place." The scene on the holy mount confirms the prophetic word, for both refer to the same thing. In other words Peter is telling us that there in the holy mount God gave a little picture of the coming glorious Kingdom. You remember the Saviour said, "There are some standing here that shall not taste of death till they see the Son of man coming in His kingdom."

And Peter says, "this voice which came from heaven we heard, when we were with him in the holy mount." Suppose we had Peter with us on the platform—I would sit down. But suppose he would not get up. Then we would say to him, "Peter, you say you saw the Kingdom there on the holy mount. What did you really see." "Oh, we saw the King. We saw Him transfigured. We saw Him in His regal robes. We saw Him in His glory, the same glory in which He will by and by appear." "And what else did you see, Peter?" "We saw a man there who had been dead for fifteen hundred years; and he was there alive in his glorified body, shining in the same effulgence as that of the Lord Jesus." "What else did you see, Peter?" "We saw another man there, and he never died at all; he had been caught up to Heaven without dying—Elijah. And he was there in the same glory with Christ." "What else, Peter, have you to tell us?" "We were there—James, and John, and I. We had not been changed; we were still in our natural bodies." There you have the two sides of the Kingdom—the heavenly side, the saints who will be raised, and the living who will be changed, caught up to meet the Lord, and to appear with Him in the glory, and with Him bear rule over all the world, and those who are living on the earth in their natural bodies are to enjoy all the blessings of the glorious Millennium age. There we have a picture of the Kingdom in miniature.

Thank God, we are moving on to the day when that will have its glorious fulfilment at the Coming again of our Lord Jesus Christ. Oh, dear friend, do not let that day take you unawares. Do not let the Blessed Lord come to you as a thief in the night, and find you unprepared. But come to Him even now, before you sleep to-night. If you are not already reconciled to Him, if you do not already have the assurance of your soul's salvation, " Kiss the Son, lest he be angry, and ye perish from the way." Bow at His feet, and kiss that pierced Hand of His in token of submission to His holy will. Receive Him as your Saviour and Lord, and know that your sins are forgiven, and that you, too, are ready to meet Him when He comes.

IV

THE HOPE OF THE CHURCH

1 Thessalonians iv. 13–18.

IT is a very interesting fact, I think, that this first Letter to the Thessalonians is the earliest of the writings of the Apostle Paul which the Spirit of God has preserved for the edification of the Church; and yet it abounds in references to the great doctrine of the Second Advent of our Lord Jesus Christ. Then, too, it was written to a very young Church. Some people are inclined to think of the doctrine of the Lord's Return as something so difficult to understand, and as a truth so deep, and so hard for simple men to lay hold of, that it should only be proclaimed to Christians who are well advanced, and who are mature in their experience, and who have a very full understanding of the divine truth. But this Church to whom Paul wrote this Letter was composed of very young Christians. Only a few months before the writing of the Letter, at the most, they had been in the darkness and ignorance of heathendom. A few, perhaps, were Jews who had been brought to a saving knowledge of Christ, but the majority of these people in the Church at Thessalonica were heathen who had been reached by the Gospel, and who were now rejoicing in Christ Jesus. Then you remember that the apostle Paul was only permitted to spend a very brief period with them. Luke speaks of his preaching in the synagogue for three Sabbath days, but how much longer he was there we are not told, possibly a little longer. Then persecution broke out, and in obedience to the Lord's word, "If they persecute you in one city, flee to another" (the apostle Paul did not then have the ultra-dispensational teacher of to-day to tell him that the Lord's words did not apply to him) he left there, and went on to Berea, and then on to Athens; and he left Timothy behind him to care for the young Church, and then to report. As a result of a letter that came to him at Athens he was so exercised that he sent Timothy back, and he could not rest until he returned the second time, and told him how well they were getting on. It was a wonderful report he brought back. Paul was fearful lest these young believers might have been disturbed by the enmity of the unbelieving Jews, and of their former friends in heathenism, who were opposed to the Gospel of Christ. But when Timothy returned he said something like this : "You know, Paul, it is remarkable the way they are going on. They are not only standing steadfast, and holding fast the Word of truth, but they are holding forth the Word of life. They have all turned preachers, and everywhere in Thessalonica they are carrying the message, and not only there but into Macedonia they have gone, and into other parts and into Achaia ; they are telling out the story with great assurance." And he must have added, "You know, Paul, they are greatly distressed over one thing. You remember you told them that the Lord Jesus Christ was coming again to reign as King." He did proclaim that truth, and persecution broke out, and the accusation was made against Paul that he was a disturber of the peace. His enemies said of him, "He is preaching another King, one Jesus." And if Paul was preaching "another King, one Jesus" then he was preaching the Second Coming of our Lord Jesus Christ. When our Lord Jesus was baptized in the Jordan and anointed with the Spirit He was set apart for three offices—prophet, priest, and king. He exercised His prophetic office here on earth. He is exercising His priestly office yonder in the glory. But He is to reign as King when He comes back again, when the kingdoms of this world shall become the kingdoms of our God, and of His Christ.

This truth seems to have gripped these Thessalonians; they revelled in it, they could think of little else. Some became so occupied with it that they were not much good for the ordinary affairs of life. There is always a danger of going too, far in regard to any truth of God, and the apostle had to give them a sobering word. What Timothy communicated to the apostle Paul was this. " Since we have been there some of them have died; they have fallen asleep in Christ, and their friends are disconsolate; they feel that they won't be here to welcome the King when He comes. They feel that they have missed so much that their hearts are really broken because of it." And Paul says, " I will just write them a Letter, and clear that up." So in the course of this Letter, he expounds the part that both those who have died before Christ's Return, and those who are living at His Coming, will have in the glorious future day. " I would not have you ignorant ", he says, " concerning them which are asleep." What does he mean by " those which are asleep " ? Does he mean when our dear ones in Christ close their eyes to the scenes of earth, when the body is dead, that we put them away, body, soul, and spirit, in the tomb, and that the whole man sleeps in utter unconsciousness until the glorious morning of the first resurrection ? No, he certainly does not mean that, because that would contradict very definitely what he taught elsewhere. Take that wonderful passage in the third of Ephesians. He says : " For this cause I bow my knees unto the Father of our Lord Jesus Christ, of whom the whole family in heaven and earth is named." Where does he locate the family of God ? In only two places—in heaven and on earth. If he were a soul-sleeper he would have said, in the grave and on earth. But he did not say that. He locates those who have left this scene as in heaven. There is not even a third place. I took up a paper in our country not long ago that stirred me to preach a sermon. It had an article beseeching the faithful to come through with more cash, because the poor souls in Purgatory are suffering so dreadfully because of the depression that has swept all over the world. And so I preached a sermon one Sunday on the subject, " What can we do for the poor souls in Purgatory ? " We had over five thousand people to hear it ; and when we got looking into the Book to find out about it, we found out that there was not any soul in Purgatory, and that the only

Purgatory there is is the precious blood of our Lord Jesus Christ, which purged our consciences from dead works to serve the living God. No, Paul does not locate any of the believers in Purgatory, and he does not leave them unconscious in the grave. He speaks of " the whole family in heaven and on earth." And you remember that elsewhere he says that the believer who dies is absent from the body—not asleep in the body—and is present with the Lord. And he says that he himself had a desire to depart and to be with Christ which is far better. How did he know that ? Was it simply the word of an inspired man who had been commanded so to write ? No, not that alone; he knew it by practical experience.

We say sometimes, No one has ever been to Heaven and come back to tell us what it is like ? We are wrong, for he had been there. He says : " I knew a man in Christ above fourteen years ago (whether in the body I cannot tell; or whether out of the body I cannot tell; God knoweth;) such an one caught up to the third heaven. And I knew such a man (whether in the body, or out of the body, I cannot tell; God knoweth;) How that he was caught up into paradise, and heard unspeakable words, which it is not lawful for a man to utter." Now, mark

you, the apostle clearly gives us to understand
there that a man can be conscious and out of the
body. For when he had this experience he says
as it were, " If I had a body, I am not conscious
of it ; and if I was out of the body, I did not
miss it ! " That helps me in regard to my friends
who have gone to Heaven. He saw and heard
something ; he was thoroughly conscious, and
he was caught up into Paradise. Paradise is a
Persian word, it is used three times in the New
Testament. It means " a royal garden." Paul
says, " I was caught up ; and I found myself in
a royal garden." I never go into one of your
beautiful English gardens without saying, " This
is a little, wee bit of Paradise." Paul found himself in a scene of ineffable beauty and glory. Then
he says, I heard something ; I heard unspeakable
things which it is not lawful for a man to utter.
So he was thoroughly conscious ; he could see
and hear. I was in a meeting down in Florida
some few years ago, and on one night each week
we used to have questions and answers. Among
the questions sent up was this one. " Will you
please tell us what the unspeakable things were
which Paul heard when he was caught up into
the third heaven." I had to admit that I could
not tell. Why Paul himself could not tell. In
other words, it was so wonderful that he could

not put it into our language. Yet he heard it at the time and understood.

Oh no, he is not telling us here that the soul is sleeping, that the spirit is unconscious. He is speaking of the tired, weary, worn bodies of the people of God, put to sleep till Jesus comes. So he says, " I do not want you to be ignorant concerning those which are asleep, that ye sorrow not, even as others which have no hope." We are not forbidden to sorrow. Our blessed Lord when He was here on earth was a Man of sorrows ; He was acquainted with grief. He looks in sympathy upon us in our sorrow. " In all their afflictions He was afflicted, and the angel of His presence saved them." We are not taught in Scripture that we must adopt a cold, hard, stoical attitude when bereavement enters our home, and snatches our dear ones away. Why, the sisters of Bethany wept at the death of Lazarus, and Jesus wept with them. He has bidden us weep with those who weep at a funeral, and rejoice with those who rejoice at a wedding. We are to enter into the joys and sorrows of one another. What He does tell us is that our griefs and sorrows are not hopeless. These people of Thessalonica, so far as this world was concerned, had no hope whatever of meeting their departed loved ones again in their

unsaved state. But to the Christians he says
regarding those who sleep in Jesus they were not
to sorrow as others which had no hope. "For
if we believe that Jesus died and rose again,
even so them also which sleep in Jesus will God
bring with him." We do believe that - don't we?
Listen to me ; if you do not believe it, you are
not a Christian. I do not know if you have any
professing Christians on this side of the water
who do not believe it, but we have some on our
side. They tell us that you can be a Christian,
and you do not need to believe in the Resurrection of Christ ; that in some way or other His
Spirit is permeating men ; that His teaching is
living after Him, and doing men good. One of
our preachers from New York, speaking over
the radio, referred to Matthew Arnold's well-
known statement when he said that the Body of
Jesus still sleeps in a Syrian tomb, but that His
soul goes marching on. People said, How
magnificent ! Magnificent nonsense ! It's a
" John Brown's body " sort of thing. If the
Body of Jesus still sleeps in a Syrian tomb, then,
according to 1 Corinthians xv, "your faith is
vain ; ye are yet in your sins." We begin with
the truth of the Resurrection of our Lord Jesus
Christ. " If thou shalt confess with thy mouth
the Lord Jesus, and shalt believe in thine heart

that God hath raised Him from the dead, thou shalt be saved." So I take it that you cannot begin as a Christian until you recognise the Resurrection of our Lord Jesus Christ. "He was delivered for our offences, and He was raised again for our justification." "For if we believe that Jesus died and rose again, even so them also which sleep in Jesus will God bring with Him," or, "will God lead forth with Him." What is He referring to ? Why, simply this, that in the Old Testament it is written, "The Lord my God shall come and all the saints with Thee." And in the New Testament He tells us the same wonderful truth. And so the Apostle says that when the Lord Jesus returns again, when He comes forth to reign, when He sets up His glorious Kingdom, He is going to bring with Him all His saints, both those who have died in the past and those who will be living at the time when He rises from the Father's throne. They are coming back with Him ; they are going to be manifested with Him in glory, and the word will be fulfilled : and " every eye shall see Him and they also which pierced Him ; and all kindreds of the earth will wail because of Him." But He will not come alone ; He will come with all His redeemed, the entire heavenly company ; those which have been put to sleep by Jesus will

God lead forth with Him. The apostle John in his Book of the Revelation, written some forty years after Paul wrote this Letter, described symbolically His Coming leading forth His saints. He pictured Him as a mighty warrior, whose Name is called the Word of God, who is clothed with a vesture dipped in blood, riding upon a white horse. And John says, " The armies which were in heaven followed Him upon white horses, clothed in fine linen, white and clean." It is a picture of the heavenly host returning with Christ to set up His heavenly Kingdom.

But how is this going to be ? You say, the bodies of our dear ones have crumbled away to dust, and their souls are with Christ, and if they are not coming back as disembodied spirits how then will God lead them forth with Him ? The apostle explains it in another verse : " For the Lord Himself shall descend from heaven with a shout." " The Lord Himself." There is something lovely about that. " The Lord Himself." I like that word—don't you ? It is not mere symbolism. He is not talking about the death angel, he is talking about " the Lord Himself." Before He went away He said to His disciples, " In My Father's house are many mansions. I go to prepare a place for you. And if I go to prepare a place for you I will come again, and receive you unto Myself, that where I am there ye may be also." You remember those two shining ones who appeared on the Mount of Olives just after Christ was taken up into Heaven. And you recall that they said to the disciples, " Why stand ye gazing up into Heaven ? This same Jesus shall so come in like manner as ye have seen Him go into Heaven." " This same Jesus." I love those words. " This same Jesus." Nineteen hundred years in the glory have not changed Him in the least. He is the same to-day as when He was here on earth. He is glorified now, but in His own Person, His character, He is the same blessed, living, loving, gracious, compassionate Lord that He was when He was here on earth. When I was a boy they used to sing in the Sunday School :

"I think, when I read that sweet story of old,
   When Jesus was here among men,
How He took little children as lambs to His fold,
   I should like to have been with Him then.
I wish that His hands had been laid on my head,
   That His arms had been thrown around me,
And that I might have seen His kind look when He
      said,
   Let the little ones come unto me ! "

Do you know how that hymn affected me ? It always made me feel that I had been born nineteen hundred years too late ; and I had an idea

that something had happened, and the Lord
Jesus was not quite the same, and that I would
never get as close to Him as those dear little
children, when they were brought to Him, and
He took them up in His arms. But I gather from
this passage that Jesus Christ is " the same,
yesterday, and for ever," and that when He
returns He will be the same wonderful Saviour
that He was when He was here on earth. And
I shall look into His eyes, and they will be human
eyes. I shall listen to the words that fall from
His lips, and they will be human lips. I shall pour
the story of my love and adoration into His ears,
and they will be human ears. I shall feel the
touch of His hands upon me, and they will be
human hands. For the Man, Christ Jesus, abides
for evermore. The Russellites and the Ruther-
fordites can have a dead, ghostly kind of a Christ
if they like, but as for me,

> " I shall know Him, I shall know Him,
> As redeemed by His side I shall stand.
> I shall know Him, I shall know Him,
> By the print of the nails in His hand."

Yes He will be the same Jesus. Why, the last
word that ever came ringing down from Heaven
before the volume of inspiration was closed, was
this, " Surely, I come quickly." And the apostle
John, speaking for the whole Church, responded,

" Even so come, Lord Jesus." This is our hope
—the personal Return of our Blessed, adorable
Saviour.

" The Lord Himself shall descend from Heaven
with a shout." Now, mark you, it does not say
that His feet are going to touch the Mount of
Olives on that occasion. That will be ; but this
is something a little different. Follow it carefully. We gather from this passage, and from the
1 Corinthians xv. that the Lord is going to
descend from Heaven, and He is coming down
into the region of the atmosphere of this earth,
and He will come with an awakening shout, and
the voice of the archangel will be heard, and the
trump of God will sound, " and the dead in
Christ shall rise first." Literally it may be ren-
dered " the dead in Christ will stand up first."
The word that is used throughout the New
Testament for resurrection is that of standing
up. I think it is something like this. Here is a
company of soldiers in a battle-field. They have
been fighting hard, and they have thrown themselves down on the ground, and they are asleep.
Suddenly the trumpet sounds, and they spring to
their feet ; and then perhaps another trumpet
sounds, and away they march. And so when the
Lord descends from Heaven with a shout, with
the voice of the archangel, and with the trump

of God, in an instant the dead in Christ stand up ; no longer are they sleeping in the dust. You say, That is an impossibility. With God nothing is impossible. If we believe that Jesus died and rose again, we need not be afraid to believe the rest of it. He was the first-fruits of them that slept. He came forth from the tomb, and the dead shall come forth from the tomb in their glorious resurrected bodies.

The Lord Jesus will descend from Heaven, and the dead will be raised, and the living changed at the last trump. There are many very earnest and sincere Christians who tell us that this last trump is the seventh trump of the Book of the Revelation, and that the Church will be on the earth all through the blowing of the trumpets of the Tribulation, and at the sounding of the last trumpet the Church will be raised. But may I say as one who can claim to have some knowledge of the teaching of this Book, for I give it the first place in all my thinking, that the Book of the Revelation was not written when this Epistle was written, and, therefore, the apostle Paul cannot be referring to the seventh trump of the Book of the Revelation. That book was not written until about forty years afterwards. And, further, he refers here not to the trump of an angel, but to the trump of God. The trumpets of the angels in the Revelation give us the various stages of the Tribulation period, and they finally come to the culmination which ushers in the Kingdom. What we, as the people of God, are waiting for is the shout from Heaven, and the voice of the archangel, and the sounding of the trump of God which will close up this present dispensation. Therefore, it is called the last trump.

What is to take place? The dead in Christ will stand up at His Coming, clothed with their resurrection bodies, and prepared to meet the King. "Then we which are alive and remain shall be caught up together with them in the clouds, to meet the Lord in the air." There will be a generation of believers living on the earth when our Lord returns. You and I may be in that generation. Those who know their Bibles best are more concerned about the signs of the times than those who do not; and we believe that the hour when this passage is to be fulfilled must be drawing very near. And we may be those of whom the apostle speaks " which are alive and remain " and who will be caught up together to meet the Lord in the air. How wonderful is the thought! Oh, the separations that death has made; the way in which it has broken families, as well as individual hearts. But when Jesus comes the dead in Christ will all be raised, and the living in Christ will be changed, and we will be caught up together to meet the Lord in the air.

People ask me sometimes, Do you think we shall know our loved ones in that day when we are caught up together? Where would be the object of our being caught up together if we did not. Here on earth we have been heirs together of the grace and love of Christ. We have had fellowship together. We have been labourers together. There should be no question about heavenly recognition. Why, there is recognition even on the part of lost souls. Jesus told of the rich man in hell who looked across the great gulf and saw Lazarus who had begged at his gate on earth, and he recognised him. And he saw Abraham, too; and though he had never seen him before, yet he recognised Abraham, and called him by name. And you remember on the Mount of Transfiguration the disciples saw that with the Saviour there were two others, and they recognised them. Nobody had said beforehand to Peter and the others, " Let me present to you our old friends, Moses and Elijah." No, the moment they looked at Moses and Elijah they recognised them. And Peter was so thrilled that he wanted to build three churches right away—

a St. Moses Church, a St. Elijah Church, and a
Holy Saviour Church. " Let us build three
tabernacles," said Peter, but he did not know
what he was talking about. But there was
recognition of the two who were with Christ on
the Mount. You know the Scripture says, " Then
we shall know even as we ourselves have been
known." Yes, we are to be caught up together,
and " so shall we ever be with the Lord." We
shall be like the Lord ; we shall have glorified
bodies just as He has. And so the dead raised,
and the living changed, will be caught up
together. That is how the Word is going to be
fulfilled. Notice it says that we are going to be
" caught up to meet the Lord in the air." This
word " meet " implies going out to meet one in
order to return with him. When I was in Aber-
deen recently I sent a telegram to a cousin of
mine telling him that we would arrive at such
and such a time, and he promised that he would
meet us. And there he was with a car waiting
for us. He came to meet us in order to take us
back to the house with him. We are going to be
caught up to meet the Lord in the air, and then
we are coming back with Him when He comes
to reign in glory for a thousand wonderful years.
The same word is used in the last chapter of the
Acts where Paul and his company landed in

Italy, and, says Paul, " when the brethren heard of us, they came to meet us " and " so we came to Rome ". We are going up to meet the Saviour, and we are coming back with Him. You say, Do you mean that we are going to live on earth in houses just as we do now ? No, our real home will be in the heavenly Jerusalem, and our relationship to this earth will be very much like that of the angels in the past dispensation, when angels appeared as God's messengers to His servants. " For unto the angels hath he not put in subjection the world to come " (or, " the age to come ") " whereof we speak." We shall be His representatives, and He shall rule the world through His saints in that day, and will appear visibly before the eyes of all people. And the Apostle concludes with this word " And so shall we ever be with the Lord." No matter what comes afterwards, we shall be with Him. I have a friend and he does not believe in this at all. He said to me one day, " My dear brother, you are going to be terribly surprised when you wake up one morning expecting to be in the Millennium and find you are in the new heavens and the new earth." I said, " I have not lost anything even if it should please the Lord to change His programme ; I shall be with Him, anyway, and that is the great thing." We are to be with

the Lord wherever He goes, and whatever He
does we are going to be associated with Him;
we are going to serve Him, and we are to have
a part in His everlasting Kingdom. Some people
have an idea that Heaven is a place of absolute
do-nothingness. When Hawthorne was over
here from America he was very much interested
in some of your old churchyards. And one day
he unearthed this epitaph:

> " Here lies a poor woman who always was tired,
> Who lived in a house where help was not hired.
> Her last words on earth were, 'Dear friends, I am
>   going
> Where washing ain't done, nor sweeping nor sewing,
> But everything there is exact to my wishes.
> For where they don't eat there'll be no washing
>   dishes.
> I'll be where loud anthems forever are ringing,
> But having no voice I'll get clear of the singing.
> Don't weep for me now; don't weep for me ever,
> I'm going to do nothing forever and ever '."

Poor thing. How tired she was! You know,
dear friends, that is not the Biblical conception
of the ages to come. It is not that we are to do
nothing for ever and ever, but " His servants
shall serve Him, and His Name shall be in their
foreheads." We shall reign with Him. We shall
bear rule with Him over a redeemed universe.
What a delight it will be to run His errands!

Let me tell you a little story. Some years ago when my eldest son, who is now Superintendent of the Coloured Bible Institute in Dallas, Texas, was a little boy, my wife, and the little lad, and myself were up in Manitoba; I was engaged there in Gospel work. And one day we left a place in South-Eastern Manitoba to go in a round-about way to the city of Brandon, where I was preaching that night, going on to Winnipeg the next morning. It was a very hot autumn day, and the men were taking in the harvest, and the people in the train were not feeling very comfortable. If the windows were opened the dust came blowing in, and the mosquitoes; and if the windows were closed everyone was half-suffocated. We stopped at a certain place, and a Roman Catholic missionary priest got on the train. (Now if there happens to be a person here, and you have been brought up in the Roman Catholic Church, do not get your back up. I expect this priest to be with me in Heaven for all eternity.) Well, he got on the train, and the dear man walked all through the car looking for a seat, but no one made room for him. Mostly the seats which accommodated two only had one person using them, but that one person was planted in the middle of the seat, and he would not move one way or the other, and so

no one made room for this priest. He was a man
of rather generous proportions, and he had on
a long dark habit, with a rope round his waist,
and a cross hanging to it ; and you can understand on such a hot day the people in the train
did not want so heavy a man pressing against
them. So at last he made his way to the rear of
the car, and he seated himself half-way on the
wood-box ; it is a place where the wood is kept
to keep the train warm. I felt sorry for him, and I
said to my wife, " There are only three of us
here ; we will get some of this luggage out of
the way, and then I will go and ask him if he
would care to come and sit with us ; it may give
me the chance to say a word to him about his
soul." So we fixed things up, and then I went
to where he was sitting, and I said, " You do
not look very comfortable there ; if you do not
mind sitting with a little family, we would be
glad to have you come and sit with us." He
said, " Thank you very much ; I appreciate your
kindness." And from his accent I knew he was
accustomed to speaking in French. So he came
to where we were sitting, and sat down. I was
anxious to get in a word with him, but it is often
difficult for me to get started with a stranger.
My mother's folk came from Rutlandshire, so
that is the English strain in me. I did not know

how to begin. We generally start with the weather, because, as a rule, there is generally some weather around that you can say something about. So I made some remark about the weather. I intimated that it was quite warm. Then he made the very original remark that they were taking in the harvest, and I agreed with him. So we got started, and finally he gave me just the opening that I wanted. " Pardon me, sir," he said, " are you a resident of our fair province, or are you just a visitor ? " " I am simply a visitor," I replied. " Are you a tourist travelling for pleasure ? " he remarked further. " No," I replied, " but I get a lot of pleasure out of it." " Are you a commercial traveller representing some business ? " he asked. " Not exactly," I replied, " though I do represent one particular house, and I have some magnificent goods to tell people about." " You excite my curiosity," he said. " Just what is your calling, if I may ask ? " " I will tell you," I said. " To be perfectly frank, I am a catholic priest engaged in missionary work." He looked at my collar ; he looked also at my wife, and little boy, and he said, " You are surely jesting with me, sir. You do not really mean that." " I was never more serious in my life," I replied, " I am a priest in the Holy Catholic Church." " You mean," he

suggested, " that you are an Anglican clergyman."
" No," I replied, " I am simply an ordinary priest
in the Catholic Church." " But you have not
the Roman collar on," he said. " I did not say
that I was a *Roman* Catholic priest," I said. " I
belong to the Church universal. I am a priest in
that Church." He looked puzzled. " I do not
quite understand," he said. " Would you like to
hear how I became a priest ? " I asked. " I would
indeed," he said. " I shall have to begin first by
telling you how I became converted." I took
two hours telling him how I became converted,
for we had lots of time. I wanted to give him
all the Scriptures, and I turned him to Scripture
after Scripture. Then at last I brought him to
the place where I came before God as a poor
sinner, and cried out to Him for salvation. And
I turned to His Word, and I read this wonderful
sentence to him : " He that believeth on Him is
not condemned." I said, " You know I saw that
the moment I believed on the Lord Jesus Christ,
God said that I was not condemned. I rested on
that, and I passed from death unto life, and He
has been my Saviour ever since." " This is most
interesting," he said. " I have never heard anything like this in my life before. You remind me
of St. Augustine." I tried to think what he
looked like, but I could not call up any effigy I

had seen. "What do you mean, that I remind you of St. Augustine?" I asked. "Don't you remember," he said, "that it was through the Book that he was converted. He had no one to talk to him, then he was told to read, and as he read the Epistle to the Romans the whole thing opened up." I said, "I am glad you reminded me of him, because it is through believing the words of this Book that I have been saved." We talked of many things, for we had all day to do it in. I told him how I learned that I was a priest, by reading the Letter by the blessed apostle St. Peter. For he said, "ye are a chosen generation, a royal priesthood." We talked and talked, and we had dinner together; and then when we reached Brandon there was a cousin of mine waiting for me, and he looked a little bit surprised as we two priests came down the steps together. I said to him, "You look after my wife and boy, and we two priests will walk along together." We talked all the time of the things of God and then we got to the junction where one road led to the monastery and the other to the Gospel Hall; and I said to him, "I am going this way, and you have to go that way to the monastery." "I wish you could spend the evening at the monastery," he said. "I should be glad to have done so," I said, "but my cousin's wife has prepared dinner for me. You are a bachelor, and you do not realise how terrible it is, when a lady has prepared dinner, for you not to be there on time to enjoy it. So I am afraid I shall have to go." "Couldn't you come up afterwards?" he asked. "No," I replied, "I have to go to a meeting." "I would like to have more conversation with you," he said. "You are the first clergyman I have ever talked with who did not get angry with me!" "Why don't you come to hear me preach at the hall?" I said. "But I could not come dressed like this," he said. "You are just my size; I have a suit I could lend you if you would care to come along to my cousin's for dinner." He laughed, and said, "Thank you very much, but I have taken solemn vows always to wear this costume." "I would not have you break your vow," I said, "and so we will have to say ' good-bye.' He took my hand, and said, "Good-bye. I have enjoyed this day. I am going to think these things over. I suppose we will never meet again." I said, "We shall meet in one of two places." He said, "What did you mean by saying, One of two places?" "In a little while," I said, "1 Thessalonians iv is going to be fulfilled." And I read to him the Scripture that we have talked about to-night. I said, "When that takes place, and it may take place at any time, I will be there with the Lord for I am going to be caught up to meet Him in the air." He said, " You are sure of it ? " " Absolutely," I replied. " Well," he said, " you must think you are a very good man." " It is just the opposite," I said. " I have been a very bad man, and I have found out that Jesus died for sinners, and as a lost sinner I trusted Him, and He washed my sins away in His precious blood. And when I am caught up to meet the Lord in the air, I shall remember our talk to-day, I will look about for you, and if your faith has been, not in the Church, not in its Sacraments, not in your good works, but in the precious atoning blood of the Lord Jesus Christ, I shall see you there, and we will have a good time together for all eternity." He was silent, and then he said, " You said ' One of two places '." " Yes," I replied, " the Scripture says concerning that event, ' Blessed and holy is he that hath part in the first resurrection ; on such the second death hath no power, but they shall be priests of God and of Christ, and shall reign with Him a thousand years.' And at the end of the thousand years, John says, ' I saw a great white throne, and him that sat on it ; from whose face the earth and the heaven fled away ; and there was found no place for them. And I saw the dead, small and great, stand before

God ; and the books were opened ; and another book was opened, which is the Book of life ; and the dead were judged out of those things which were written in the books, according to their works '. Now," I said, " when that event takes place, I will be there. I shall not be in front of that throne for judgment, for my judgment was dealt with when those two arms were outstretched on Calvary's Cross, and when the weight of my sins fell upon Jesus, my Substitute, and by trusting in Him I have been saved from judgment. And wherever He is His saints are going to be with Him. And if I have not found you in the air when Jesus comes, I will look for you there in that great throng, and if you have lived and died depending on the Church, and the creeds and sacraments of the Church, and on your good works to save you, I shall see you there, and I shall see the awful look that will come over your face as the Blessed Saviour has to say to you, " Depart from Me, ye cursed, into the everlasting fire prepared for the devil and his angels." " God forbid ! Not that ! " he cried out. " It need not be," I said, " if you will trust that precious blood of Jesus to wash away your sins. Is it to be Christ, or the Church, and your good deeds, and your prayers ? In what do you trust for salvation ? " He was silent ; and then he looked up with tear-filled eyes, "Christ, He is the Rock" he said. "I dare not trust in any-one but Him. I rest my soul on Him." "That is what St. Augustine said. Not Peter, but Christ is the Rock on which the Church is built," I said. "If that confession comes from your heart, then I shall see you in the air when Jesus comes."

Are you trusting the Lord Jesus? Are you ready to meet Him when He comes? If you have never availed yourself of what He did the first time when He was here you will never be ready to meet Him when He comes the second time. He died to put away sin, and if you trust Him to-night you will be saved for eternity, and ready to meet Him when He returns.